Crow Speak

Wild Poems

Gail Galloway

2020

Published by Ashwood Books 2020

Text copyright © 2020 Gail Galloway

This edition copyright © 2020 Ashwood Books

This book is sold subject to the condition that it shall not by way of trade or otherwise, be lent, resold, hired out, or otherwise circulated without the publisher's prior consent in any form or binding and without a similar condition including this condition being imposed on the subsequent purchaser.

First published in Australia October 2020 by Ashwood Books.

PO Box 73, Franklin, Tasmania 7113

www.ashwoodbooks.com

ISBN

Print 978-0-9874111-7-4

Epub 978-0-9874111-8-1

Typesetting by Jonathan Sturm

Printed and bound in Australia by Lightning Source.

National Library of Australia Cataloguing-in-Publication Data. A catalogue record of this book is available on request.

Ashwood Books

For Melanie Lea

A dedication to all my crow sisters
and family
who shared my journey over time,
including the years these poems unfolded.

The author acknowledges the traditional owners and custodians of country where she has lived, walked and worked. In places that inspired these poems: The Bundjalung, Gadigal, Githanbul, Goomeroi and Wiradjuri people of NSW and Melukerdee and Luggermairrenerpairer (Palawa People) of Tasmania.

Acknowledgements

Special thanks to:
Peter Harris, long and loyal friend, who at the very least, prodded me back to the writing desk to realise this book.

Also to Judith Harris for adding her elegant art.
Heart felt appreciation.

Katherine Lomar and Christine Porter for their professional advice and encouragement. The small happy adventures and long meandering phone calls from friends supported the creative journey. As a poet, Katherine's input in particular over the course of my writing life has been valuable.

To my proof readers—for their sharp ears and eyes, especially John Wilson (The Alternative Academy) for his quality critiques in the final creative flurry to finish.

In closing, a nod to Jonathan Sturm—a special kind of genius, early mentor and friend for supporting my emerging craft (and first novel) in the late 1990's, and now completes a circle, as publisher of this collection. A great gratitude.

This collection contains two previously published works.
'In Sacred Places' original version in *Small Packages#7*
(New Century Press, 2003) QLD.
'Temptation' in Famous Reporter 30, literary biannual
(Walleah Press, 2004) TAS.

Illustrations

Original works by Tenterfield artist Judith Harris—images in charcoal and pastels.

Photographs by Gail Galloway.

Contents

One	1
Crows Feet	2
Two	3
Sunday	5
A Blackbird Song	6
Calvary	7
Acid Drops	8
Edge of Extinction	9
Road Rage	10
A Carcass Called Economy	11
Owl Passing	13
Omen	14
Upwardly Mobile	15
This is Not a Poem About Crows	17
Temptation	19
In Sacred Places	21
Forest Ravens	22
Night Watch	23
Sun Talk	25
Mating Advice	26
Crow Speak	27
Endnotes	28
About the Author	29

One

Today, only one is stationed in the tree outside
and wakes me just on dawn.

Bellow-like lungs pump.
Arrk, arrk, arrk, aaaragh: I count the remarks.
The last word drops off the scale.

From a distance further, comes a gurgled retort.
He arks up again.
This one has a lot to say and huffs out a few more paragraphs.

He chants — some sorcerers conjure:
complex instructions,
travel notes,
a weather forecast,
or just some long yarn about the neighbour?

The closing lexicon is met with a melodic chortling.
A dry laugh.
Downstream
a distant bark floats.

I wait for another peeling.
There are no more interjections.

Mirth and sun wrinkled
eye lines. A story clawed in
crows feet

Two

As earth takes her first breath,
I am bundled, barefoot in a blanket

on the front step,
to watch the light ascend.

Dawn is still.
The sun bends to kiss the stratus,

when overhead
two dead straight lines cut the air.

An old couple in slow conversation
strike for the horizon.

Night hangs on their wings.
They've come from a long way back.

I eavesdrop as they pass,
hear their rasp voices saw, back and forth.

Its been a hard haul
Their pitch falls lean.

In parallel time, they trawl
a cool wash of sky.

Perched, all ears
keen to decipher their tongue;

I scry on bones for wisdom;
a drift of undertone; some tale of passage.

I am an unborn child,
trying to reap the meaning of exchange.

But all I catch, is the scoop of wings
pushing back air.

Sunday

They were knocking about in the scrub
under trees blackened from fire,
scratching earth.

A couple rushed at me, arched up,
open beaks yellow,
a warning screech.

I don't belong to their congregation,
a strange grubbing church.
My own conviction wavers.

They gather for communion,
some intoxicating ritual
where their high order keep me at bay.

While in wait, I hold my heart:
for their octave bark is a killing hymn.
I had wanted some part.

Yet as they circle in on prey,
those sleek coats and eyes brim glee.
I catch a glint of what — I can not say.

Remember how they clawed the dirt;
their courtly guard
a mass of bellicosity.

I will not wager with their unholy tongues:
the murder of crows
and their stolen suns.

A Blackbird Song

Protest for all Aboriginal deaths in custody

Sing a song of Serco,*
a paddy wagon drive,
a six and forty black man
slowly baked alive.

When the case was opened,
the press began to sting.
But human rights don't count for much
when justice means nothing.

* Serco is a private security company implicated in the Inquest into the (2005) Death of Mr Ward, Coroners Court of Western Australia, 2015.

Wagga Wagga, NSW

Calvary

They raised a cross for the coming and going near the Murrumbidgee
where I was born, in a Waradjari place of many crows.

The maternity ward was demolished later for a parking lot,
when they added extra storeys to improve turnaround.

To raise more souls, just down Hebron Way from Bethlehem,
outside the walls of Jerusalem,

the dead poor and crucified remains were
left for the birds at Calvary. Early Christians raised a story

and a church there to idolise their tortured son
and package misery to the masses.

My uncle raised funds for a cancer ward at Calvary Hospital,
(a private place) in Wagga, but my aunt and cousin, both died

all the same. We don't expect any resurrections from there,
but plenty of crows, still haunt the sky.

Drops of uric acid.
Birds leave graffiti—
painting white statues

Central Plateau, Tasmania

Edge of Extinction

By nightfall we made camp at the Steppes,
close to where the bushfire had burnt,
up to a thin edge of Eucalypti.

A small vestige clings to life
by the bitumen.
It feels desolate.

Some big trees remain amongst the survivors,
wide grey girths creak. These great ancestors
are silent now. Waiting for death.

There is only one bird call in the night.
A lonely crow,
voice keened with loss.

In this place, where diversity once flourished,
stands a circle of sculptures in stone and bronze.
A memorial for lost species.

My mind wheels back to an earlier time
when we chanced here in light rain, to find
bright boughs, a flush of natives in dance.

Hard to imagine now,
that in just over thirty years
we have brought nature to her knees.

Channel Highway, Tasmania

Road Rage

Rounding a bend with a grudge
of politics on my mind,
a raven crosses my path:

Swoops the road in front,
a wing dips the bituman,
the other tilts a—'fuck you'
finger at my fender.

The corvid skims vision,
(almost hovering)
and blocks my rumination.

A sleek of body
glints blue green. A sheen
of iridescence that stops my breath.

With pointed intent
the stealth bomber
wheels down, bumps to land
muscles flexed,

sun white on its back.
All geared up as it hops over
to inspect a roadside carcass.

A Carcass Called Economy

(After Terra Nullius)

Then Eden was almost lost. In the fall
of trees and blackened koalas, our cities smoked.
Heads locked in the dragon's jaw,
our faces burnt. It was summer after all.

On highways torn, TV drove political heat.
Amongst the carnage we glimpsed a carcass
not unlike the average road kill
except it came from Capitol Hill.

The first horseman arrived shortly after.
Here was a moment to pause and reflect.
But not for long, memory is short.
Too many mourned the loss of sport.

Dozed in the ever-hot sunshine of this ancient land,
he who pays the FIFO's calls the tune.
The white noise of amnesia is the only mantra
in habitats where forests bleed and suburbs sprawl.

To build our carbon nests, we let the cull of songbirds be.
Different brands of invisible friend chant support
in a chorus line for the urban poor:
'We will all be saved by spending more.'

Spoils are spent, all fuel traded. As data charges
fast asleep on beds of straw,
we clutch the reigns of a horse called war.
'Because we're all in this together.'

We sell arms to eat while Syria's children wait
at gates, or in detention to keep them safe.
Its about development after all,
with project funds to help our mates.

Over 200 years of white supremacy,
now strapped to the back of a drone, a last horseman
spurs on the gas led recovery. Don't moan —
'Because we're all in this together.'

There are still waterholes to poison and once
the last artifacts are blast:
we forget the genocide,
collective good,
or that consumption was once a disease.

Just count on the economy —
because we are the digital caste,
and *'we're all in this together.'*

At the end of ecology
will we remember
how we sacrificed nothing — to have it all?

Owl Passing

The ants had already begun their funeral march
around your wide eyes.
Dear solemn creature,
the shock of loss is hard to capture.

I found your fawn feathers downed,
a small corpse laid bare—one who
sees no future, knows no rapture.
Incensed the trees cried out for our poor raptor,
lent their leaves for a shroud of fumes.

So we smoked you a goodbye,
weaving a blue scent for you
smelling the gum and resin—I lay
calling the clay,
while crows watch and wing
away.

Moon shadows wave your distant breath
once with me strong—sage
in thanks I gave your life
to the tree and stone
dead.

I walk in knowledge
with you gone,
day's memory is far and long.
The brightness too clear
to feel
or touch
your name inside me.

Omen

Sometimes you will find one
a dark feather
speared to ground
A perfect blade
plunged from sky.
Divine
this thin edged reality
The crow's gift
A knife
to cut illusion
from blind eyes.
A message stick
to guide.
It lends energy
a winged strength
Revere
The firmness of plume
its curved shape.
Learn its irony
of vanes
the barbs.
Strong spine—
a hollow
clue
to know
your own
bones.
Reflect
how to discern
between
delusion and hope
and if hope is
faith or
faith
is fantasy.
Know
what to hold
and when
is time.
Let go
allow
past
to
fall

Upwardly Mobile

There you were, ironing your shirts
and hanging them inside the tree trunk.
It was an odd little house we shared,
in that small, one up, one down flat,
with barely room to swing a cat.

Your white work shirts, I worried
would rub against the bark,
dirt the sleeves with earth or sooty ash
where the fire had lapped.

But you laughed—silly!
showed how you stored pressed clothes
in a downstairs room
the size of a cupboard.

Once upon a time,
as young lovers with
our first rental nest in the city,
we were babes in the wood.

You, so well groomed in urbane style,
even back then, in that faraway house.
Later you would move on to higher places
while I flew north and south.

In better company, moving up
on your well heeled path—
an early adopter of mobile phones.
The trunk call an echo—
our childhood past.

Now in a leafy crescent,
two point one, with your goodly wife,
have your own home
in a better suburb, in a better capital.

Why would I dream—of visiting you
in such a strange abode
in a big tree in that smokey city?
This I ponder, while making do

in muddy boots and furry hat.
Down here where I have more room
to spread my wings.
The air is better and my nearest neighbours
all wear feathers.

This is Not a Poem About Crows

for the million birds killed daily by cats

You have mistaken their protective vigil by your bed
for loyalty: this is merely a guise.
They know your every move and how to elude you.

Programmed to care, you are blind to their sins.
TV sets channel the ideology of subservience,
Purr, Friskee, Desire: you want the best for them.

You stroke the soft folds of their belly.
Do not be fooled by the shared moments of intimacy,
they merely pretend love and sleep,

disappearing through the walls of your dreams
to visit other beds. The opportunists return
to greet you at dawn.

Wake with the smell of sweet blood on their teeth.
Smile. Toxoplasmosis spreads from their shit—
you happily clean up. It's a measure of your love.

You don't expect them to return the favour
because they just have clumsy paws.

Pinned to your chest with mass defying gravity,
their hypnotic glass eyed gaze,
you mistake for love.

It is a well crafted trap they lay,
the heavy heart and numbness of limbs—
feelings subjugated by Cheshire grins.

They whittle down your boundaries with those claws,
little by little, in tiny meows and delicate whiskers
nosing into your arms, engine purring.
They are your guilty pleasure.

Deep down you know they are a killing machine
but suffer the little deaths — moths,
small marsupials and coloured birds.

Graduating from ground dwellers.
You forgive these slain offerings,
mere gestures of love.

Ignore their climbing thirst. You know
they can take down a crow
to skull brains for a nightcap.

So willingly feed small morsels of your soul
to stave off the day they turn on you.

Temptation

Before dawn
I bake myself
sweet pie (a single serve)

This temptation
to poke dates
add extra spice, some pip

4.20 am: blackbirds screech
frost the window.
Pain cracked and

missing—my companion
the old schnauzer,
his stinking hair mats

my dressing gown
measures the circumference
of plates rattled

dreams of buttery scrolls
like tops of Doric temples
Curling ash thin hair

the woolly shuffle of feet, dandruff
pads on cold linoleum, scuffed.
I sift resentment

with salt and flour
to powder my face,
prepare to fill the case

my lungs huff warm
smoke billows
the chimney stacks

Wait. My pastry skin flakes
over hot oven—
I have eaten half my age in weight

hoist this frump arse up to the fire door
hope it melts me like a candle
(fat chance)

one sliver; a slice
clove spikes
my tongue, prone to embellish

The pie
I feel it glow,
plump in my belly

Woolool Wooloolni, NSW

In Sacred Places

where mountain lowry keep their colours
the dash of red and green, orange wings splash recall
where the lizards crawl to dream between afternoon clefts
spiders weave their secrets between tree trunks, pin
coded messages to rough bark and under stones
where bandicoots burrow to hide their stripes
in these small places we can wake our own dreaming,
breathe the musky scent of possibility
that bursts from seed pods in the space
where knowing sleeps   crow observes all

Forest Ravens

Before storms blacken,
they flock the hillside.
From the treetops, ravens wheeze.

Their heavy breath rasps
a slow alarm
before thunder crack and wind blast.

Foggy chords play the slopes
and wurrs the valley.
It sounds of squeezebox.

Diadem St, Lismore, NSW

Night Watch

A humid evening. Dusk sheds a heavy scent.
The gum tree is full
as a bar before close time.

A chorus of blackbirds
pitch a quarry of constant vowels,
to herd in the night.

They share a strange alphabet
and scatter it, in cryptic song circles
around my bed.

Raucous talk is hard to follow.
One long diatribe is a struggle to read but
the chant, rhythm and news, soon dims out light.

Then a few take operatic parts.
From the Eucalypt, a hush falls
as one calls a lullaby.

Zeds fall on my pillow.
I catch the tail-end of a verse,
but the next chapter is a complete mystery.

One by one, dark missives drop.
When dawn slips in, there is a whistle stop.
The night-watch

ratchets off a few guttural notes
in a redundant language—
it signals the end of a long shift.

I wake much later—find everyone gone:
the sun too high, my eyes a scrabble,
head is a tumbled nest.

Nothing to crow about.

Sun Talk

A language with imaginary friends, cultured barefoot in the bush.
I cut a nasal voice from wire grass, followed sheep pads to creek beds
where early seeds of thought were muttered only with the birds.

Time found a circle where social lingo was learned. A country kid
around sheds, I squatted with the blokes, whose mumbled yarns spilt
from sides of mouths. Mostly men of few words, they smoked
in rolled up sleeves, arms brown: some used sticks to draw on ground.

Just so you get the picture. As if I, like Icarus, was too close to the fire,
Mum would call me away, "Leave the men to talk"
But their drawling stories had already made a mark.

I was sent for elocution to be better understood.
These lessons to improve my speech, taught to open mouth,
lift my tongue, and with articulated lip, speak as a young girl should.

I've talked my way into many places since, (into and out of trouble),
in towns where proper nouns are melted, names with meaning
lost on sons with little sense of pronunciation.

I miss the old men and their stories, most now gone to ground. Yet
landscape still communicates, the baking bones give cadence
found in lazy vowels, a pitch and tone that sticks to mind.

Perhaps it is why, I listen out for ornithological tales. The slack
and slow, ululated sighs of crows.

Four Mile Creek Rd, Tenterfield

Mating Advice

They say crows do not sing...
When you landed, I was a single bird too.
Yet knowing you had pecked the eyes of newborn lambs
and rapped my gutters just for fun,
were you a survivalist or a sociopath?

You collected stones to drop like bitter truths.
Once you had trawled my garbage,
chewed the scraps of my former life, I like to think
we made a feast of that lonely time together.

There was never a rattle or coo from you
but your mocking gaze told me:
Five seconds of sex was far too long with him
and in future to discern when seduction
involves too much growling.

Belongil Lagoon, Byron Bay, NSW

Crow Speak

Would you still want to know me if I had told you
I was talking to the crow that day?

You merely glimpsed the tail of raven conversation,
and thought I was speaking to you.

Barely overheard, I repeated nothing when asked.
My words told only for the bird, black and true.

On turned wing with piercing eyes, the juror spied,
as we had our way in the sun rolled dunes.

What I said then — was over your head. Up on
the limb, where the witness hovered by.

Uttered back in salted air, a feathered prose.
It was not for you, my voice — that way.

Those words intoned were not for you to prey.
My reply was to the brooders question.

The answer is not for you. It is not for you
to know when crow speaks.

Endnotes

Pg 6. With respect to the deceased's family. A Blackbird Song: at the time of writing there were at least 441 deaths of First Nation People in custody. This being 25 years since the 1991 Royal Commission into Aboriginal Deaths in Custody, which recommended a number of systemic changes to address the problem. It is argued that to date, few of these have been introduced.

See: https://www.aic.gov.au/publications/sb/sb17

Pg 7. Calvary: Once widely known as place of many crows, the NSW City of Wagga Wagga took its name from a Wiradjuri word.

It is now recognised the Aboriginal place name was an erroneous (colonial) translation with the true meaning of the term being Dance Dance or place of many celebrations.

In August 2019, Wagga City Council acted on the evidence of Stan Grant Senior, local elder and author of the first Wiradjuri dictionary. Adopting the more festive definition, the city is now going through a re-branding process as part of their Reconciliation Action Plan.

Pg 11. Edge of Extinction: FIFOs. An acronym used to describe the fly-in, fly-out workforce — employed predominantly by mining companies in Australia. This is a practice of contracting FIFO tradespeople, often from urban or regional areas and flying them into remote sites. For corporations this is preferable to employing or training a local workforce.

We're all in this together song by Benjamin Lee, the tune became popularised as a solidarity call during the Covid lockdowns of 2020.

About the Author

Gail is a rural Australian writer and artist. She has worked as a journalist, social worker and community activist. Focused on themes of social justice and environment, her poems range through the personal to the political. Some of her earlier works have been published in anthologies and magazines, *Crow Speak* is her first collection. She also gardens, grows garlic and fails to keep the house tidy. Her next book *Confessions of a Homegrown Herbalist*, (non fiction) will be published by Balboa Press.

She Tweets as *mediagal64*.

Printed by Libri Plureos GmbH in Hamburg, Germany